I0191123

Also from Westphalia Press
westphaliapress.org

Dogs in Early
New England

Dogs in Early New England: Colonial Canines
All Rights Reserved © 2017 by Policy Studies Organization

Westphalia Press
An imprint of Policy Studies Organization
1527 New Hampshire Ave., NW
Washington, D.C. 20036
info@ipsonet.org

ISBN-13: 978-1-63391-631-9
ISBN-10: 1-63391-631-6

Cover design by Jeffrey Barnes:
jbarnesbook.design

Daniel Gutierrez-Sandoval, Executive Director
PSO and Westphalia Press

Updated material and comments on this edition
can be found at the Westphalia Press website:
www.westphaliapress.org

Dogs in Early New England

Colonial Canines

by Howard M. Chapin

WESTPHALIA PRESS
An Imprint of Policy Studies Organization

DOGS

IN

EARLY NEW ENGLAND

BY

HOWARD M. CHAPIN

PROVIDENCE
PRESS OF E. A. JOHNSON & CO.
1920

DEDICATED

TO THE MEMORY OF

PETER

who taught me to love dogs and inspired
this study into their history

Dogs in Early New England

By HOWARD M. CHAPIN.

Dogs have from the earliest times been domesticated even by the most primitive races, and have had a marked influence upon the thought and literature of mankind; yet when one thinks of Colonial New England, with its austere Puritans, one is too apt to picture a dogless society, and to forget that even in that harsh theocracy, pioneer dogs strove, as did their masters, with the rough hardships of a struggling civilization.

Even before the Pilgrims came to New England, two English dogs,[1] "Foole" and "Gallant" by name, "great and fearefull mastives," the chronicler tells us, landed in 1603 upon the shores of southern Massachusetts, where they nosed and smelled about the beach and shrubbery, exploring and investigating unknown scents and smells. After the false alarm of an Indian attack, in which turmoil "Foole" grabbed up a half-pike in his mouth, the dogs with their human companions returned to Martin Pring's bark, the "Discoverer," and sailed away. These were, as far as we know, the first European dogs to set foot upon New England.

The "Mayflower," on her famous voyage in 1620, brought two dogs, a mastiff and a spaniel,[2] to New England. These two dogs were permanent settlers, not transient explorers like "Foole" and "Gallant." As dog pedigrees and stud books go back, unfortunately, only to the early nineteenth century, none of the blooded dogs of today are able to trace their descent from the dogs that came over in the Mayflower.

Mourt recounts some of the hardships of these four-footed Pilgrims as follows:

"These two (John Goodman and Peter Browne) that were missed, at dinner time tooke their meate in their hand, and would goe walke and refresh themselves, so going a little off they finde a lake of water, and having a great Mastiffe bitch

---

[1]Purchas his pilgrimes, Edit. of 1625, vol. IV, p. 1656.
[2]Mourt's Relation, 1622, pp. 27, 28 and 29.

2

with them and a Spannell; by the water side they found a
great Deare, the Dogs chased him, and they followed so farre
as they lost themselves and could not finde the way backe,
they wandred all that after noone being wett, and at night
it did freeze and snow, . . . and another thing did very much
terrifie them, they heard as they thought two Lyons[3] roar-
ing . . . so they stoode at the trees roote, that when the
Lyons came they might take their opportunitie of climbing
up, the bitch they were faine to hold by the necke, for she
would have been gone at the Lyon,"[4] and under the date of
January 19, 1620-1:

"This day in the evening, John Goodman went abroad to
use his lame feete, that were pittifully ill with the cold he had
got, having a little Spannell with him, a little way from the
Plantation, two great Wolves ran after the Dog, the Dog ran
to him and betwixt his leggs for succour, he had nothing in
his hand but tooke up a sticke, and threw at one of them and
hit him, and they presently ran both away, . . ."[5]

It appears that previous to the arrival of the English, the
Indian has domesticated the dog, for in November, 1620,
Governor Bradford notes that Captain Myles Standish, on his
reconnoitring expedition on Cape Cod, met a party of Indians
with a dog.[6] Roger Williams in his "Key" gives the Indian
name for the dog as Anum, with the accent on the last syllable.
He adds that this is the pronunciation in the Coweset dialect,
but that it varies as Ayim, Arum, and Alum in the Narragansett, Quinnippiuck, and Nipmuc dialects respectively. In
Woods' "New England Prospect" we are told that the Indians
believed that "at the portall of their Elysian Hospitall, lies a
great Dogge, whose churlish snarlings deny a Pax intrantibus
to unworthy intruders."

An Indian dog gave the alarm of the English attack on the

---

[3]i. e., wild cats.

[4]Mourt, pp. 27 and 28, under date of January 12, 1620-21.

[5]Mourt, p. 29.

[6]Bradford's History of Plymouth, p. 48, also see Glover M. Allen's
"Dogs of the American Aborigines."

Williams' Key, ch. XXXII; Woods' N. E. Prospect, pt. 2, ch. 19.

DOCTOR HUNTER'S DOGS BY GILBERT STUART

This is considered Stuart's earliest work extant. It is now owned by Mrs. William E. Glyn of Mayfield, Newport, a descendant of Dr. Hunter. Reproduced through the courtesy of Mrs. Glyn.

Copper hair ornament, found in the Indian graves at Charlestown, R. I. Now in the Museum of the Rhode Island Historical Society.

Pequot Fort in 1637; Mason's description of the incident being as follows:[7]

"There being two Entrances into the Fort, intending to enter both at once: Captain Mason leading up to that on the North East Side; who approaching within one Rod, heard a Dog bark and an Indian crying Owanux! Owanux! which is Englishmen! Englishmen! We called up our Forces with all expedition, give Fire upon them through the Pallizado; . . ."

Thus it will be seen that dogs were serving with the Indian forces in 1637, and although not as highly trained perchance as the canine warriors of the great World War, yet these early dogs were doubtless as diligent and serviceable as the times and circumstances permitted. A somewhat similar instance occurred at Cocheco in 1689 when the barking of a dog aroused Elder William Wentworth just in time to prevent a surprise Indian attack. This dog's warning saved the Wentworth garrison, the other four garrisons at Cocheco being taken by the savages.[8]

Nothing has been discovered to show that the English used dogs in the earlier Indian wars, but by the time of Queen Anne's war, they used dogs as regular auxiliary. A report in regard to the operations of the English in Hampshire County, Massachusetts, in August, 1706, reads:

"We are just sending out 50 Men with Dogs, who are to divide into small parties, and range the Woods on both sides the River (near Hartford), if possible to discover and annoy the Enemy."[9]

But to return to the subject of Indian dogs, we find specific references to the dogs of the Connecticut and Narragansett Indians[10] in 1658 and 1661, respectively, and also we find that the Narragansett Indians used rough drawings of dogs as personal signature marks in 1644[11] and 1660.[12] They also had

---

[7]Mason's Pequot War.

[8]Wentworth genealogy, vol. 1, pp. 97 and 98.

[9]Boston News-Letter, August 12-19, 1706.

[10]Prov. Town Papers 0121; Prov. Town Records, vol. 3, p. 7; and New Haven Town Records, p. 358.

[11]Gorton's Simplicities Defence, p. 160, mark of Tomanick.

[12]R. I. Land Evidence, vol. 1, p. 88, mark of Towasibban.

implements ornamented with figures of dogs. A stone pipe ornamented with a dog carved in relief was found in an Indian grave at Burr's Hill, Warren, Rhode Island,[13] and a copper hair ornament, with two dogs in relief as the chief decorative design, was found in an Indian grave at Charlestown, Rhode Island.[14] The latter may be of a foreign design and received in trade. The killing of noncombatant Indian dogs in Queen Anne's war only serves to illustrate the brutality of human beings.[15]

Dog laws were enacted at an early date in New England, Salem having passed one in 1635.[16] The dogs' chief offences were killing sheep[17] and swine,[18] biting horses[19] and cattle,[20] spoiling fish[21] and entering Meeting Houses[22] during service. The latter offence being explained by the fact that they could not understand the sermons and simply wanted to find their masters.

Their attacks on other animals were often directly instigated by human beings, as when Mr. Verin's maid set her dog on Mr. Brown's goats;[23] when Samuel set his dogs "to the pullinge of the tayles" of John Leech's cows;[24] when Mrs. Rowden hunted cattle with her dog[25]; when Joseph Billington

[13]Now in Museum of the American Indian, Heye Foundation, New York.

[14]Now in Rhode Island Historical Society Museum, Providence.

[15]Boston News-Letter, February 10-17, 1706.

[16]Salem Records, p. 40; Jamestown Proprietors' Records, vol. 1, p. 66; Portsmouth Records, vol. 1, p. 223.

[17]Mass. Col. Records, vol. 2, p. 252; New Haven Town Records, p. 233; R. I. Col. Records, p. 22, mss.

[18]New Haven Town Records, pp. 170, 171, 246; Prov. Town Records, vol. 3, p. 125; Essex County Court Records, vol. 7, p. 273.

[19]New Haven Town Records, pp. 470 and 471.

[20]Prov. Town Records, vol. 3, p. 7; Prov. Town Papers 0121; Salem Court Records, vol. 1, p. 19; Essex County Court Records, vol. 1, p. 174; New Haven Town Records, p. 358; Austin's Geneal. Dict. of R. I., p. 85.

[21]Salem Records, p. 130.

[22]Salem Records, vol. 2, p. 210; New Haven Town Records, p. 233, vol. 2, pp. 156 and 355.

[23]Salem Court Records, vol. 1, p. 19.

[24]Essex County Court Records, vol. 1, p. 174.

[25]Essex County Court Records, vol. 2, p. 101.

Indian pewter pipe found in excavations at Montague, N. J. Reproduced through the courtesy of the Museum of the American Indian, New York.

Roger Williams in Chapter 6 of his "Key" says of the Indians that "They have an excellant Art to cast our Pewter and Brasse into very neate and artificiall Pipes."

hunted Edward Gray's ox with a dog,[26] and when Thomas Langden and his dog killed Mr. Prudden's hog.[27] Even the drastic Massachusetts dog law[28] of 1648 recognized the fact that the dogs were not always really to blame, but were often "set on" to such acts by human beings.

Dog derivatives served as ship-names and place-names in New England,[29] and also the words[30] "dog" and "puppy" were used as terms of reproach, as they are today.

Reference has already been made to the part that dogs played in military service. We find that their usefulness in other lines was also recognized legally, even by our self-centered Calvinistic ancestors. In 1648 the Colony of Massachusetts Bay[31] authorized each town to purchase hounds for use in the destruction of wolves. The town of New Haven voted in 1656 to purchase some mastiffs[32] from "Stratford or Long Island, where they here (hear) is some," to be used as auxiliary to the militia. During the interim before these dogs arrived, twelve local dogs were drafted temporarily into the service of the town. The names of the owners of these dogs are given.[33] This is the first recorded list of dog-owners in New England. Governor John Winthrop[34] and Governor John Endicott[35] were both dog owners. Roger Williams wrote in 1669 in regard to Governor Winthrop's dog, "I have no tidings (upon my enquiry) of that poore dog (about which you sent

---

[26] Austin's Geneal. Dict. of R. I., p. 85.

[27] New Haven Town Records, pp. 170 and 171.

[28] Mass. Col. Rec., vol. 2, p. 252.

[29] Salem Records, p. 163; Plymouth Colony Records, July 6, 1640; Commerce of Rhode Island, vol. 1, p. 47.

[30] Essex County Court Records, vol. 1. p. 256; Steuart's "Some Observations," etc., p. 64; New Haven Town Records, p. 46; Narragansett Hist. Reg. IX. p. 63.

[31] Mass. Col. Records, vol. 2, pp. 252 and 253.

[32] New Haven Town Records, p. 291.

[33] Mr. Gilbert, Jer Osborne, Edwa Parker, John Cooper, William Bradley, Will Tompson, Fran. Newman, Phill Leeke, Mr. Gibbard, Edwa Perkins, John Vincom.

[34] Mass. Hist. Soc. Col., series 5, vol. 1, p. 414; Narragansett Club Publications, vol. 6, p. 332.

[35] Mass. Col. Rec., vol. 1, p. 197.

Indian stone pipe, unearthed at Burr's Hill, Warren, and now preserved at the Museum of the American Indian, Heye Foundation, New York. Reproduced through the courtesy of the Museum.

At the Sign of the Greyhound, near the church, in Williams Street, Providence, 1772.

10

Signature mark of the Indian
Tomanick, 1644.

Richard Waterman's Seal.
1729.

to me. I feare he is run wild into the woods, though tis possible that English or Indians have him. Oh, Sir, what is that word that sparrows and hairs are provided for & numbered by God? then certainly your dog & all dogs & beasts."

In 1644 a Medford dog rescued Mrs. Dalkin from drowning.[36] Governor Winthrop wrote in regard to this:

"One Dalkin and his wife dwelling near Medford coming from Cambridge, where they had spent their Sabbath, and being to pass over the river at a ford, the tide not being fallen enough, the husband adventured over, and finding it too deep, persuaded his wife to stay a while, but it was raining very sore, she would needs adventure over, and was carried away with the stream past her depth. Her husband not daring to go help her, cried out, and thereupon his dog, being at his house nearby, came forth, and seeing something in the water, swam to her, and she caught hold on the dog's tail, so he drew her to the shore and saved her life."

The abuse and maltreatment of dogs by human beings was of course common in early New England. Two cases due to religious fanaticism are worthy of notice. In 1644 at Salem,[37] John and Stephen Talbie were admonished for "unbecoming speeches" about a dog in the water, but "the baptizing of him" was "not proved," although apparently charged by the authorities.

On Tuesday, April 23, 1706, somebody fastened a cross on the head of a dog, and for such a flagrant display of papist sympathies, the poor dog was beaten and killed by Captain Dudley's boatswain.[38]

On the other hand we have instances of persons being tried for abusing and killing dogs.[39]

The first case of rabies[40] in New England was observed in 1763, according to Ezra Stiles.

---

[36]Winthrop's Journal under date of 1, 21, 1643-4; vol. 2, p. 162.
[37]Essex County Court Records, vol. 1, p. 65.
[38]Samuel Sewell's Diary in M. H. S. C. 5, VI, 159.
[39]Essex County Court Records, vol. 2, p. 6; vol. 7, p. 424; Mass. Col. Rec., vol. 1, p. 197.
[40]Stiles' Itineries, p. 487.

In the realm of art we find that the earliest extant work of Gilbert Stuart is the picture[41] of two of Dr. Hunter's dogs. In 1729 a seal engraved with the design[42] of a running dog and the word "Canis," was in use in Providence.

Hannah Robinson's spaniel "Marcus"[43] figures in the sad romance of that ill-fated South County beauty.

In this connection, one is reminded of Shepherd Tom's[44] remarkable account[45] of the barking of South County dogs which could be heard for four miles. He wrote:

"What seemed stranger to the old man than all was the barking of a big watch-dog some two miles away, across the river, at the old brick house then owned and occupied by Amos Gardiner, and which is yet standing. Nichols said that the watch-dog to the east of the hill, apparently, never barked but in response to the baying of a foxhound that was roaming in a big wood lying not less than two miles to the westward and northward of where he stood, making a distance between the two animals some four miles, with the McSparran elevated hill intervening. Of this fact he felt tolerably sure, as there were occasionally lengthy intervals when both dogs were quiet, which were never broken until the hound uttered his howl, which was on the instant replied to by the hoarse bark of the distant watch-dog."

The Providence Gazette for November 7, 1772, informs us that Nathaniel Wheaton on Williams street, in Providence, used a greyhound as his shop sign, and gives us a picture of it. Ten years later the same newspaper contains a curious advertisement which reads:

"A DOG LOST

Strayed away, or more likely to have been seduced to follow some persons, or stolen, a Spaniel D O G, of about a middling Size, pyed with a white and brownish Colour, with

---

[41]Mason's "Stuart," pp. 5 and 6.

[42]Manuscript deeds in Library of Col. George L. Shepley at Providence.

[43]Hazard's "Recollections of Olden Times," Chapter VI.

[44]Thomas R. Hazard.

[45]Hazard's "Recollections of Olden Times," Chap. XVI.

shaggy Hair, hanging Ears, and docked Tail; particularly he had a white Strip in his Face, a white Ring around his Neck, and about an Inch of the Stump of his Tail white; he answers to the Name of SPRING, is very good-natured, and easy to be seduced by those who use him kindly to follow them or their Horses.—Whoever will bring or send back the Dog to me, his Master, in Providence, shall be very handsomely rewarded.   TERENCE REILY

Providence, February 22, 1782."

In the following decade, too, the same newspaper has a similar advertisement which is as follows:

"STRAYED
in Providence,

A Red and white spotted POINTER DOG, with a tolerable long Tail, had on a Brass Collar, with the Owner's Name, JOHN FRANCIS, engraved thereon, and the word "London, 1791;" he answers to the name of PONTO. Whoever will leave Information with the Printer, so that the Owner may recover the Dog, shall receive FOUR DOLLARS Reward.

N.B. Said Dog has been seen at Exeter, in this State.

Providence, Sept. 23, 1791."

The late Samuel Adams Drake in his "Old Boston Taverns" mentions two signs bearing pictures of dogs. The Greyhound, he tells us, was a tavern in Roxbury, and the Dog and Pot in Boston at the head of Bartlett's Wharf in Fish (otherwise known as Ann or North) Street. The illustration of the later sign is taken from Drake.

These few references from the fragmentary and meagre records of early New England serve to show that dogs played no small part in the lives and thoughts of our Colonial ancestors.

DOG AND POT.

(From Drake)

www.ingramcontent.com/pod-product-compliance
Lightning Source LLC
Chambersburg PA
CBHW071943020426
42331CB00010B/2991